EARLY ISLAMIC CIVILISATION

Catherine Chambers

W

FRANKLIN WATTS
LONDON•SYDNEY

First published in 2014 by Franklin Watts

Copyright © Franklin Watts 2014

Franklin Watts
338 Euston Road
London, NW1 3BH

Franklin Watts Australia
Level 17/207 Kent Street
Sydney, NSW 2000

Editor in Chief: John C. Miles
Editor: Sarah Ridley
Art director: Peter Scoulding
Series designer: John Christopher/White Design
Picture research: Diana Morris

Dewey number: 956

Hardback ISBN 978 1 4451 3408 6
Library eBook ISBN 9781 4451 3407 9

Printed in China

Franklin Watts is a division of Hachette Children's Books,
an Hachette UK company.

www.hachette.co.uk

*In this book, we have used the abbreviation pbuh (peace be upon him) when mentioning the
name of the Prophet Muhammad (pbuh) to show respect.*

CONTENTS

WHERE DID IT ALL BEGIN?

In 632 CE the Holy Prophet Muhammad (pbuh) died in Madinah, a desert city in Saudi Arabia. The Prophet spent his life encouraging Arab tribes within his region to believe in one god, Allah. He also inspired them to love learning, discovery and creativity. After his death, his followers created the Islamic civilisation — one of the greatest in the world.

4

Mosques

It was important for all Muslims to construct a mosque wherever they settled. Here, Muslims could gather together to worship Allah, to learn, to discuss their faith and sort out community matters. The Prophet himself designed the first mosque near Madinah, from which all others take their main shape and purpose. The first mosques were open-air and made of sun-baked clay walls and palm trunks. A shaded courtyard space offered travellers and the sick a place of rest and recovery.

Islam in the Golden Age

After the Prophet's death, religious rulers called caliphs spread Islam far and wide. These caliphs ruled over realms called caliphates. The first was run by the Umayyads, whose capital was Damascus in Syria. They established Islamic territories as far west as North Africa, Sicily and Spain. But by 750 a second caliphate became dominant. This was ruled by the Abbasids, whose capital was Baghdad in Iraq. Under their leadership it became the glistening cultural heart of Islam.

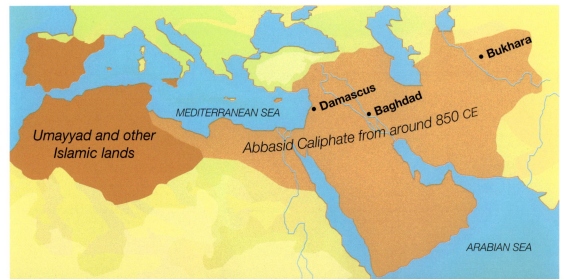

This map shows the rough extent of the Abbasid Caliphate and other Islamic lands from around the mid-800s CE – modern-day countries covered by this map area include Iran, Iraq, Syria, Jordan, Saudi Arabia, Egypt, Tunisia, Morocco, Spain and Portugal.

MEDITERRANEAN SEA

• Damascus
• Baghdad
• Bukhara

Umayyad and other Islamic lands

Abbasid Caliphate from around 850 CE

ARABIAN SEA

5

The Dome of the Rock in Jerusalem was built in 691 CE and is the oldest surviving mosque. It was built on the rock from which Prophet Muhammad (pbuh) ascended to heaven to receive messages from Allah.

The evidence

How do we know about Islamic civilisation in the first three centuries after the death of the Prophet? We know a lot from written texts and inscriptions made on artefacts and architectural features. Under Islam, the Arabic alphabet and script developed to record the life and teachings of the Prophet. Later, Arabic was used for writing poetry, scientific research and discoveries, histories, travels and trade.

 ## Around the world

c. 3000–1460 BCE Pakistan/India
Archaeology tells us about the Indus Valley's great cities such as Mohenjo-Daro and Harappa. But for the moment we know nothing about the first rulers.

c. 3000–30 BCE Egypt
Archaeology and hieroglyphs tell us about ancient Egypt. Pharaoh Namer was the first king of a united Egypt around 3000 BCE.

900 CE West Africa
We know about the origin of the Kingdom of Benin through archaeology and oral, or spoken, history. Ogiso Igodo was the first Ogiso, or king.

WARFARE AND WEAPONS

The first Islamic military campaigns after the Prophet's death were waged by his father-in-law, Caliph Abu-Bakr. Foot soldiers and horse or camel cavalries then expanded the Islamic empire through Arab lands and far beyond.

6

Weapons of style

Islamic armies were well organised by trusted generals, who were given large territories to administer once they had been conquered. Early Islamic generals fought firstly with a mix of familiar, local weapons. Later, Islamic weaponry developed its own identity. It was lightweight, strong and lethal. It included razor-sharp sabres, daggers, maces, cutlasses and axes, with stylish, highly decorated handles.

This long, slender sword with its hilt (handle) of gold, silver, ivory, pearls, rubies and turquoises is from the 15th century. But it resembles the lethal shape of earlier Muslim weapons.

Cutting edge

Skill with the bow and arrow was highly prized, especially when archers fired their arrows from a galloping horse. This particular skill improved even further when Turkish slave soldiers arrived. The Abbasids brought in these excellent horsemen to help defend the caliphate. It was a decision that they were later to regret (see pages 28-29).

Early Islamic caliphs and generals built strong fortresses to defend their territories. This one, at Arg-é-Bam in modern-day Iran, was destroyed by an earthquake in 2003.

Deadly beauty

The power of early Islamic weaponry lay in its materials. The Syrian city of Damascus was famed for the steel used to make swords and daggers. 'Damascus steel' or 'watered steel' was prized in Europe for its strength and sharpness. Its wavy pattern was a sign of its quality and durability. The effect was created during the smelting process in crucibles, which were white-hot earthenware ovens.

🌐 Around the world

c. 3000–30 BCE Egypt
Pharaohs have great stocks of weapons. Some of these are copied from their captured enemies. The khopesh – a thick, curved sword – is horribly effective.

c. 1600–1460 BCE China
Shang Dynasty armies fight with bronze weapons and fast-moving horse-drawn chariots.

c. 900 CE Central America
Mayan kingdoms fight wars with each other using stone clubs and arrows with tips made from glass-like obsidian. Sometimes Mayans resolve conflicts through 'peace talking'.

ORDER AND ORGANISATION

This aerial photo shows modern-day Baghdad. The city's position on the River Tigris was vital for trade and defence, as well as providing a constant supply of water.

This reconstruction artwork shows the walls around 10th-century Baghdad. Each ring of walls could be defended separately.

By the mid 700s, the Abbasid caliphs had stamped their power across a wide region. All they needed now was a capital city from which to run it. It was important for them to build something grand — a symbol of central power and tight organisation.

Building Baghdad

The Abbasid Caliph, al-Mansur, rejected the Umayyads' capital, Damascus. In 763, he chose instead to build Baghdad on a flat site on the great River Tigris, in modern-day Iraq. It was well placed along existing trade routes and its climate was healthy. Over 100,000 architects, builders and craftsmen worked on the city. They came from all over the Muslim world and from different faiths. Abbasid caliphs encouraged this diversity.

Strength and power

Baghdad was also known as *Madinat al Salam*, the 'city of peace'. But it was designed to draw the eye to the strong power base at its centre. To this end, it was planned in three rings, with a huge mosque and the caliph's palace at its heart. Two broad avenues linked four massive gates, and a moat surrounded it. Outside the city's core, bustling markets and industries indicated the city's commercial importance.

Cutting edge

Caliph al-Mansur ruled the Abbasid Empire firmly, and according to strict Islamic law. This law covered everything from family matters and land disputes to taxation. But al-Mansur broke away from earlier rulers' use of Arab administrators. Instead, he chose capable, well qualified men from across the empire. They became judges, advisors, ambassadors, generals and wazirs. A huge network of clerks and officials supported their work.

9

Around the world

c. 3000–1460 BCE Indus Valley
Indus Valley cities are built of baked clay. Their grandest buildings and widest streets are often set up high on mounds. Narrower streets lie below.

900 CE Kingdom of Benin
The king's palace is surrounded by a thick clay and wood wall and a deep ditch. This, and the whole city, lie within an outer wall and strong gates.

900 CE Central America
The Mayans build grand cities, palaces and temples from large, shaped stone blocks. Amazingly, they use only stone or flint tools to cut and chisel them.

LIFE IN BAGHDAD

Baghdad was well known for its splendid buildings made from large blocks of marble and stone. Its streets contained houses with highly decorated balconies and roof terraces. This style is known as *Shanasheel*, which refers to the elaborate windows.

A city of skills

Further from Baghdad's centre, the streets narrowed. Clusters of kiln-baked and sun-baked brick buildings housed manufacturing industries. The city thronged with bakers, carvers, metalworkers, jewellers, leatherworkers and many other highly skilled artisans. They sold their goods in busy markets and organised themselves into associations called guilds, which kept standards high.

10

Beating the heat

Shanasheel windows were first recorded in Baghdad as late as the 1100s. However, the design had developed earlier in Islamic Spain, where skilled craftsmen pierced intricate patterns into wood or stone windows. These were often built on three sides, with a cushioned window seat inside, and a shelf for unglazed water pots. Breezes blowing through the pierced windows cooled both the water in the pots and the room.

There are still traditional shanasheel houses in Baghdad today. Their sunny balconies and latticed windows are often finely carved. Inside, there is a cool, private courtyard.

Cool place to be

Baghdad around 900 was an international city, much like London and New York are today. People were drawn to it from all over the caliphate. They enjoyed its wide streets fanning out from the centre and visited its shopping arcades filled with luxury goods. Busy government officials, scribes, translators and merchants wandered through peaceful watered parks and flower gardens.

A busy covered market, or bazaar, in Isfahan, Iran. Today bazaars are still a central feature of cities across the Islamic world.

Around the world

c. 3000–30 BCE Egypt
Artisans such as coppersmiths, goldsmiths, basket weavers, perfumiers and potters live in quarters on the edge of cities such as Memphis. Many work for the pharaoh.

c. 1600–1460 BCE China
Workshops for bronze workers, stonemasons, jade carvers and other artisans are built near the royal palace. The workers live in small houses nearby.

900 CE Kingdom of Benin
Each group of skilled bronze workers, wood and ivory carvers and cloth makers lives in their own quarters within the city walls. They are organised into guilds.

TRAVELLING ACROSS THE CALIPHATES

Travel was the lifeblood of the early Islamic Empire. Boats called dhows carried goods and passengers to ports around the Persian Gulf and East Africa, making long-distance journeys relatively easy. Meanwhile, caravans of heavily-laden camels criss-crossed desert sands.

12

This modern dhow is built to a traditional design, and is capable of carrying very heavy goods. It is shown cruising near Zanzibar, an important East African early Islamic trading port.

A thirst for travel

Roads and pathways from Persia to Spain were teeming with travellers on foot, horseback or on donkeys. These travellers included scholars, religious teachers, geographers, ambassadors and tourists as well as merchants. The Muslim tradition of hospitality meant that they were welcomed and given food and shelter along the way.

Cutting edge

Large dhows with crews of 30 were perfect for shipping trade goods along the eastern Indian Ocean and through the Red Sea. Wheeled carts were useless across the sands and rocks of the Arabian Desert and the Sahara but the camel was just perfect. Its broad feet easily coped with heavy loads and sinking sands.

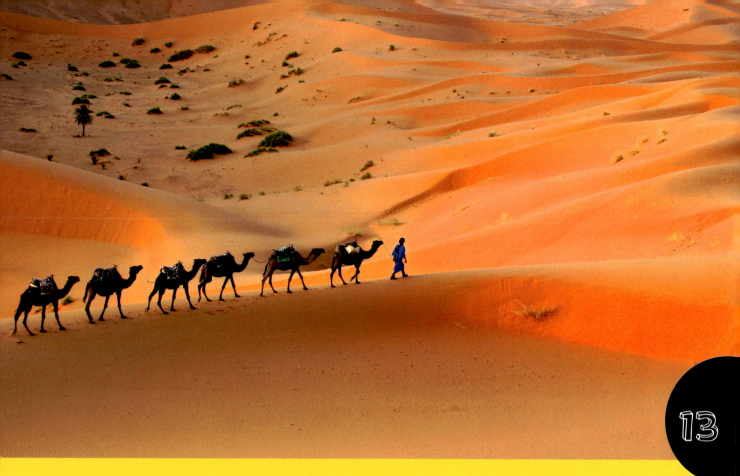

Travel writing

Travel led to the first true tourism and travel writing. Wealthy tourists took part in a Grand Tour, a *Jawla*, and were given the respected title, *Jawwal*. At first, travellers narrated their accounts to spellbound audiences. Then, they became diaries that were included in the works of intrigued scientists. By 1100, the *rihla*, the first true travel writing, was published. Since then, great Muslim travel writers such as Ibn Battuta (1304-1377) have given us a window into the medieval Islamic world.

Camel caravans like this crossed the Sahara, where great Islamic trading settlements such as Sijilmasa emerged. The western trans-Saharan trade in salt, gold and leather was very valuable.

 ## Around the world

c. 3000–1460 BCE Indus Valley
Indus Valley settlements are built near the great Indus River, so many traders and travellers use boats. People walk or use carts over mountain passes.

c. 3000–30 BCE Egypt
Small boats made from papyrus and large wooden ships carry trade goods, travellers and the pharaoh's ambassadors. Pack animals such as camels are used across desert lands.

900 CE Kingdom of Benin
Benin's traders carry lightweight goods on their heads along a network of forest pathways. Large canoes transport heavier goods and soldiers along creeks and rivers.

WHERE TRADE GOES, ISLAM GOES

The gold coin below is a Syrian dinar. It dates from 698-699, and its inscription is in Arabic. The coin's date tells us that even in the first decades of Islam, Islamic trade was healthy. By the time of the Abbasids, trade networks had expanded across the now-vast Islamic lands.

14

A wealth of goods

For centuries before Islam, goods from as far as China had reached right across to Europe along the so-called Silk Road. In early Islamic times, caliphs controlled this trade as soon as it reached their territory. In Baghdad's shopping arcades, the wealthy could buy silk, linen, printed cloth, furs, precious metals and stones, spices and slaves.

Trade and faith

Each time this coin changed hands, the message of Islam was spread. Teachers of Islam often travelled with the caravans, too. Islam took hold along trade routes deep into the southern Sahara. It was known even as far as Scandinavia, where Muslim traders bought precious furs.

This Syrian gold dinar has the Muslim declaration of belief in Allah – the *Shahada* – inscribed on it. The inscription reads, 'There is no god but Allah and Muhammad is the messenger of Allah.'

This picture shows a caravanserai, a protective fortress and stopping point for Islamic merchants and travellers. Here, animals could be stabled and goods sold or bartered. This caravanserai is in Anatolia, Turkey.

Postal orders

A strong banking system developed among early Islamic trading nations. This meant that letters promising payment were honoured all the way from Baghdad in the East to Portugal in the West. The Abbasids also introduced a postal system that helped merchants to communicate with each other. But the Baghdadi caliphs used it as a spy network, which included spying on the merchants!

 Around the world

c. 3000–30 BCE Egypt

Goods are bartered. But grain and oil are also used as a type of money. These can be stored and used in times of famine. Some peasants get rich on storing them.

900 CE Kingdom of Benin

Traders sell cloth, spices and elephant ivory and other goods to neighbouring kingdoms. Their currencies are cowrie shells and brass bracelets called manillas.

900 CE Central America

Mayans barter their cloth, pottery, feathers, ornaments, bells and precious stones such as jade. Their long trade routes link North and South America.

SCIENCE REACHES THE STARS

The elaborate brass object in the main picture is an Arabic astrolabe dating from the 900s. Astrolabes were used in both astronomy and astrology – just two of the many sciences studied by enthusiastic early Islamic scholars.

16

A thirst for knowledge

The quest for trade, travel and pure enlightenment thrust forward science, mathematics, geography and medicine during the early Islamic period. Scholars sought knowledge from China to India and from Persia to Spain. Baghdad became a great centre of learning. The city's 'House of Wisdom', completed by Caliph al-Ma'mun in 813, attracted scholars of all faiths.

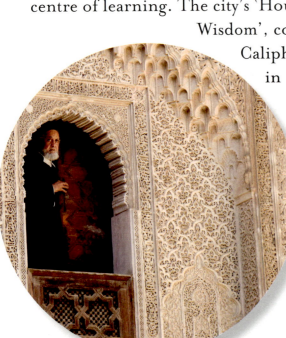

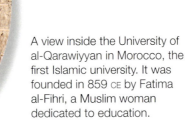

A view inside the University of al-Qarawiyyan in Morocco, the first Islamic university. It was founded in 859 CE by Fatima al-Fihri, a Muslim woman dedicated to education.

Islamic Spain introduced the astrolabe and other navigational instruments to Christian European sailors, enabling them to find their way more accurately.

Cutting edge

The astrolabe could measure the universe in three dimensions. Together with the quadrant, it helped tell both time and distance. For Muslims, they also pinpointed the *quibla* – the direction of Makkah to which they prayed.

Star gazers

Developments in mathematics made new instruments far more accurate. Early Islamic mathematicians hugely improved algebra and trigonometry. This in turn pushed forward knowledge of time, space and distance. Mathematicians such as al-Battani (850-929) revolutionised *zijs*. These were numerical tables listing the positions and movement of the Sun, Moon and fixed stars, and coordinates within the solar system.

17

 ## Around the world

c. 3000–30 BCE Egypt

Architects use a measuring rod to design huge pyramids. Farmers measure the Nile flood's depth with them. Mathematics and the decimal system are developed.

c. 1600–1460 BCE China

An early type of porcelain is invented during the Shang Dynasty, and other crafts such as bronze making advance greatly. Astronomers develop a calendar based on the cycles of the Moon.

900 CE Central America

Mayans develop complicated arithmetic of their own and understand the importance of 'zero'. They tell the time through the movements of the Moon, Venus and constellations.

FAITH WRITING

The page below from the Holy Qur'an shows the most important function of Arabic writing. This was to record the Word of Allah, as revealed by Archangel Gabriel to the Prophet. In Early Islamic states, Arabic became vital for trade, administration and learning.

Spreading the Word

The written Qur'an, and another set of writings called the Hadith, enabled all Muslims to understand and study their faith. During early Islamic times, Arabic was standardised. This meant that it had to be written using rules of grammar that everyone could learn. So teachers, scholars, traders, travellers, administrators or soldiers could communicate easily across the empire.

This page from the Qur'an was handwritten in the late 800s or early 900s.

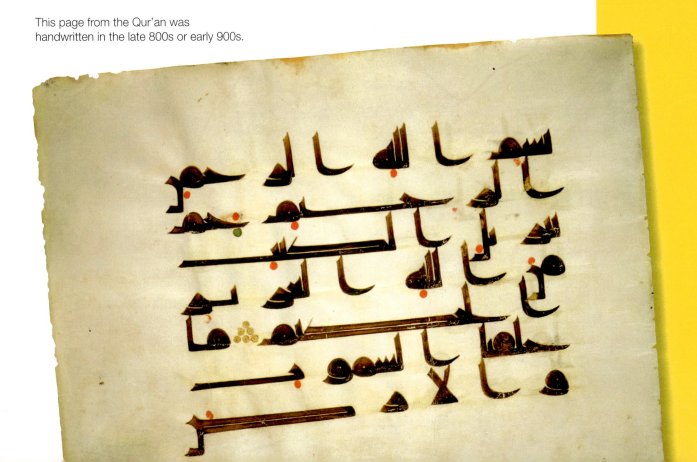

Craftsmen and artists used Arabic words and phrases to decorate pots, fabric and buildings, as here in the plasterwork of the Alhambra in Spain.

Reading the script
Each line of the Holy Qur'an is read from right to left, with every page written in elegant Arabic script. The picture on the left-hand page shows the early Kufic style. There are many others, but they all show 28 different consonants. There are no symbols for different vowel sounds, but small dots indicate where vowels should be. Other dots help the reader to distinguish between consonants that look similar.

Beautiful and practical
Early Islamic scribes wrote in ink, watercolours and gold, and used pens rather than brushes. They worked on sheets of parchment, made from dried animal skins. Later, they adopted paper technology from ancient China, but refined the paper's texture with a coating of starch paste. Sometimes, writing surfaces were dyed with deep colours such as indigo blue. Gold lettering made a sparkling contrast.

Around the world

c. 3000–30 BCE Egypt
Ancient Egyptians developed hieratic (cursive) writing and numerals, which were written by priests on papyrus and walls. Hieroglyphs (picture writing) uses picture forms as well as symbols.

c. 1600–1460 BCE China
Shang Dynasty writers inscribe symbols on bronze, and on oracle bones, which are used to predict the future. These early writings confirm what later writers say about the Shang Dynasty.

c. 900 CE Central America
The Mayans develop an advanced form of writing called Zapotec. It records flourishing farming and the profits from bustling trade. Mayans record their history, too.

WONDERFUL WATER

Islam spread from the deserts of Arabia to many other dry, rocky lands. So water was always precious and the desert oasis was seen as a green jewel in the sands. Early Islamic cities such as Baghdad were built or expanded along other natural waterways, such as rivers and hot springs.

Eram Garden in Shiraz, a city in Iran, was built in the mid 1800s but has many older design features. Eram comes from the Arabic *Iram*, which means 'heaven'.

20

Irrigating the crops

Water was essential for irrigating food crops, and Early Islamic engineers designed elaborate watercourses for farming. Baghdad was built along the wide River Tigris, so its citizens had a constant supply of water. But with a population that reached over half a million by 900, the city needed irrigation to grow crops on the nearby river floodplain's fertile soils. So Baghdad's engineers built a system of canals that ran along high banks. These canals also served as protective ramparts.

Tiling became popular in homes and mosques throughout the Islamic world in the 10th to 11th centuries. Patterns showed complex geometry, such as here, or beautiful floral and leaf patterns.

21

Gardens of paradise

Beautiful flower gardens with fountains and trickling streams were also important in early Islamic cities. These gardens were taken from descriptions of paradise gardens in the Holy Qur'an. But many were influenced by pre-Islamic Sasanian design. This featured a plot divided into four quarters by streams; each quarter was planted with flowers and shade trees.

Cutting edge

Islamic tiles like the ones shown above shine and shimmer in water. They lined the public and private bathhouses, or hammams. We do not know exactly when tiled bathhouses were first built. We do know that by the 800s, Baghdad alone had around 5,000 of them. Hammams hummed with workers, from the dung collectors who provided fuel to heat the water to stokers, water carriers, robe keepers and skilled barbers.

 ## Around the world

c. 3000–1460 BCE Indus Valley
The great Indus River supplies endless water. Homes in the major cities have shower rooms where the water drains into large clay-pipe sewers.

c. 3000–30 BCE Egypt
The Nile floodwaters are drained into basins and then into canals. Machines such as the shaduf then irrigate the crops.

900 CE Kingdom of Benin
Large Benin houses have courtyards where rainwater runs into underwater storage systems. Water is purified in huge pottery jars using herbs.

A BURST OF FLAVOUR

22

The main picture shows a plate made for the table of a wealthy family. It represents the importance of dining well in early Islamic civilisations. At that time, Islamic scientists improved farming tools, irrigation and flour milling techniques used by other cultures. In this way, food production increased.

Celebrity chefs

Imported foods such as rice from India, sorghum from Africa, and fruits, vegetables, herbs and spices helped to create Baghdad's distinctive food tradition. We know a lot about the dishes enjoyed by the elite through Ibn Sayyar al-Warraq's book, *The Book of Cookery Preparing Salubrious Foods and Delectable Dishes*. It was written in about 950 but is a collection of recipes from the caliphs' kitchens in the 800s.

This glazed bowl dates from the 900s and comes from what is modern-day Iran. Later patterns were more complex and colourful.

A world of flavours

Early Islamic cooking gave us many flavours and recipes. Ibn Sayyar al-Warraq's recipe book included a carrot smoothie, flavoured with ginger and honey. Carrots were a favourite ingredient and came in reds, yellows and whites. They were used a lot in puddings, like khabis. This set custard was made with milk, honey, eggs and carrots, flavoured with cloves, nutmeg, ginger and cassia, which is like cinnamon.

Desert foods

The food culture of the desert, where Prophet Muhammad lived, remained important to Muslims. Meals of sheep, goats, milk, dates, figs, grapes, pomegranates, honey, barley and wheat bread were timeless ingredients for many. All Muslims are required to fast between sunrise and sunset during the month of Ramadan. The tradition of breaking the fast by eating three dates, was and still is, popular.

Dates are the fruit of the date palm, shown here. Dried dates were and still are an important desert food that gives energy. They can be easily transported without spoiling.

23

Around the world

c. 900 CE Central America
Mayans grow maize as their main crop. They also eat cactus, greens, beans, rabbit, turkey and fruits.

900 CE Kingdom of Benin
Benin lies in thick forest, where animals are hunted. Rivers and creeks provide fish, such as the mudfish. Yams are the staple crop.

c. 3000–1460 BCE Indus Valley
Farmers grow wheat that is made into flat bread. Most people eat grains, vegetables, salted sea fish, and river crocodile.

FINE FABRICS

The fabric fragment in the picture below is from a silk shawl, from about 900 CE. There is little written information on fabrics from this early period. But survivals like this show fine quality with vibrant colour and attractive design.

This beautifully woven silk shawl comes from the Islamic city of Cordoba, in Spain. Islamic Spain developed its own silk industry, so silk no longer had to imported from the Far East.

24

Islamic fabrics like these are made from camel hair and have long been used to keep nomadic traders and herders warm. They are richly patterned with natural dyes.

Magic carpets

Baghdad had such a large population that it had to import thousands of rugs and carpets from eastern Persia. Some designers continued the early Sasanian tradition of dividing the rug's pattern into four quarters, rather like their gardens. But newer Islamic motifs such as the crescent moon, star, flowers, fruits and vegetables were applied.

A world of cloth

Many early Islamic cloth fragments have been found in Egypt, Yemen and elsewhere, but they were most likely made in Baghdad. Fabrics include a surprising mix of linen, cotton and rabbit fur. Others are plain linen, or linen and wool mix. They are painted or stamped with repeated wood-block patterns, or panels of Arabic script.

25

Fashion divide

There were differences in fashion between East and West; between the Abbasids of Baghdad and the Umayyads of Sicily, Spain and North Africa. But generally, men and women wore plain or patterned long tunics over wide trousers. Long shawls or hooded cloaks covered women's shoulders and sometimes their heads, while men wore a turban or a close-fitting cap. Fine filigree gold and silver jewellery were prized accessories.

 Around the world

c. 3000–30 BCE Egypt
Egyptians grow flax along the banks of the River Nile. It is woven into long, white, lightweight strips of linen cloth. Pigments from earth and rocks dye cloth for the rich.

c. 900 CE Central America
Mayans weave material from bark, cotton and the hemp plant. They embroider animal symbols such as the snake, and long bands showing the stars and planets.

900 CE Kingdom of Benin
Benin is famous for its cotton cloth, dyed with natural pigments. Women weavers make it in different thicknesses and in plain, striped or more complex chequered patterns.

PLEASURE AND LEISURE

**Islamic instrument makers developed the *oud*, or lute —
the stringed instrument in the main picture. Composers
set poetry to music, creating unique musical forms. These
songs were made to entertain the wealthy. But music and other
pastimes spread to the streets right across the Islamic world.**

26 Pastimes for princes

The horse was ridden for pleasure as well as battle, so Baghdad's elite took up
the ancient Persian game of polo. A 10th century historian, Dinvari, wrote that
'a player should strictly avoid using strong language and should be patient and
temperate'. These qualities meant that polo, as well as music, backgammon and a
form of chess called *shatranj* were all part of a wealthy boy's education.

This is a shatranj set made of highly glazed
pottery. It dates from the 1100s. Shatranj was
a form of chess played during the early Islamic
period, although the game is much older.

Instrument makers developed the oud, shown here, flute, bass drum, guitar, sitar, early violin, castanet, and others. These were based on earlier Arabic instruments.

Mixing the music

Classical Islamic music developed from older Arab, Persian and Byzantine styles, with influences from Africa, too. The music of the desert fused with urban music to produce new sounds, and Baghdad became a centre for this new kind of music. Islamic musicians wrote books of song and musical theory.

27

Songster

Al Ziryab, which means 'the blackbird', was a famous singer and musician in the 800s. He was born in Baghdad but was probably of African descent. At the Spanish Islamic court, Al Ziryab added a fifth string to the oud. He also used a vulture's quill on the strings instead of a wooden plectrum, to change its sound.

 ## Around the world

c. 3000–1460 BCE Indus Valley
We know that Indus Valley peoples love dancing through dance poses sculpted in stone, bronze and terracotta. Stringed instruments, some like harps, are played.

900 CE Kingdom of Benin
Guilds of musicians play stringed instruments, hand clappers, bells, drums, flutes and horns. Court musicians accompany historians as they narrate deeds of past kings.

c. 900 CE Central America
Mayan musical instruments include flutes, panpipes, whistles and ocarinas that are shaped like animals. There are rattles, and drums made of wood or pottery.

DEATH AND DECLINE

Muslim burials are based on simplicity and purity. But there are grand Islamic mausoleums such as this 10th-century example from Bukhara city, in modern-day Uzbekistan. Inside lies the tomb of Ismail Samani, the founder of the Samanid dynasty at the end of the 800s. Bukhara was one of the cities that began to rival Baghdad.

28

Death of an empire

During the 900s, Abbasid rule over the Islamic world started to fracture, and Baghdad lost some of its power. African and Turkish slaves and slave soldiers, called Mamluks, started to rebel. North African territories pulled away from the Abbasids. However, in Spain, the grand Umayyad court at Cordoba continued to flourish. Baghdad's position at the heart of Islam turned to dust when the Mongols from Asia overthrew the Abbasids in 1258.

Ismail Samani's tomb, shown here, is made from highly patterned brickwork. The walls are so strong that they have never needed repair.

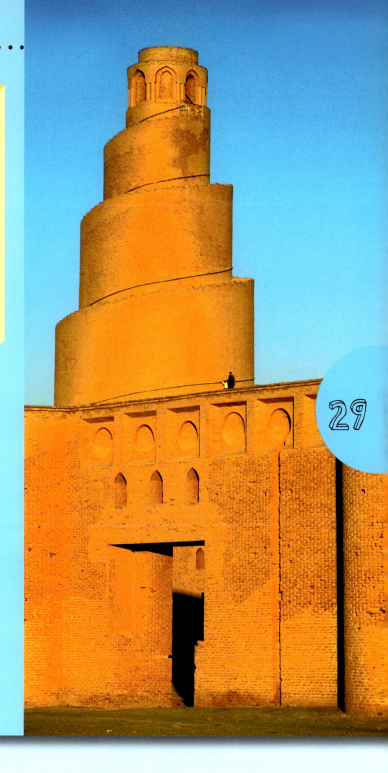

A place in heaven

To reach paradise, it is not enough for a Muslim to be buried according to Islamic customs. Muslims have to do good in this life. In the early Islamic golden age, caliphs and governors made sure that there were hospitals, lodgings for weary travellers and help for the poor. In Baghdad, skilled workers' guilds also provided shelter for travellers, care for orphans, and money to set up schools.

Beautiful tombs

Baghdad's ancient mausoleums have long gone. But we can get an idea of Abbasid tomb architecture in cities such as Bukhara. Many tombs are brick built and feature a dome. Elaborate, patterned brickwork and finely pierced stone windows show the skill and money lavished on those buried inside.

The Great Mosque of Samarra, in modern-day Iraq was built by the Abbasid Caliph, Al-Mutawakkil in the mid 9th century. Samarra became a temporary capital for the Abbasid caliphs.

 ## Around the world

c. 4000–2000 BCE Sumer
Ancient Sumerians are buried in the ground to be closer to other human souls. Sumer declines in 750 BCE when the city walls of Ur are battered by Amorites.

c. 900 CE Central America
Mayans are buried with maize in their mouths to symbolise their souls' rebirth. Bodies are sprinkled in red mineral dust, the colour of death, then wrapped in cotton.

900 CE Kingdom of Benin
Benin kings are buried in their ancient spiritual homeland city of Ile Ife to the north west. Benin declined in the 16th century and was ransacked by British forces in 1897.

GLOSSARY

Ambassador A ruler's representative in another country.

Artisan Skilled, expert craftsman or craftswoman.

Astrolabe Instrument for measuring the position of the stars, planets, Sun and Moon to calculate time and distance on Earth.

30

Astrology Study of the galaxies, Sun and Moon to predict the future.

Astronomy Study of the planets, stars, galaxies, Sun and Moon.

Barter Exchange goods rather than pay for them with money.

Caliph Islamic religious leader and political ruler.

Caravan A company of merchants or pilgrims travelling together with their animals.

Crucible Earthen pot used as a very hot oven, or kiln.

Dhow Sailing boat with triangular sails used by Arab traders to transport heavy goods.

Dinar Unit of money used across Islamic lands.

Hadith Collection of the deeds, sayings and teachings of the Prophet Muhammad (pbuh).

Jawla Grand Tour taken by rich Islamic tourists across many lands.

Kufic First Arabic script with many styles.

Oasis Natural patch of wetland in the middle of desert.

Oud Muslim lute.

Qibla Direction in which Muslims must face to pray, often indicated in a mosque by a niche called a mihrab.

Quadrant Instrument that helps calculate distances by measuring angles up to 90 degrees.

Rihla Muslim travel writer.

Sasanian Referring to an empire and people that existed in the area of modern-day Iran before the arrival of Islam.

Silk Road Ancient trade and cultural links from China to the Mediterranean.

Sorghum Grass types that provide cereal.

Steel Very hard metal made from iron ore and carbon used for sword blades and many other objects because of its strength.

Trigonometry Mathematics that measures the relationship of lengths and angles in triangles to calculate distance.

Wazir Islamic Minister, or advisor to a ruler.

Zij Numerical table used in astronomy to calculate the positions of the planets, stars, Sun and Moon.

WEBSITES

You can learn basic facts about Islam on:
http://www.bbc.co.uk/religion/religions/islam/ataglance/glance.shtml

Find out more about Islamic art on:
http://www.bbc.co.uk/religion/religions/islam/art/art_1.shtml

Take a look at Islamic architecture on:
http://www.bbc.co.uk/religion/religions/islam/art/architecture.shtml

You can find out about Islamic Spain, which developed at the same time as the Abbasid empire on:
http://www.bbc.co.uk/religion/religions/islam/history/spain_1.shtml

Note to parents and teachers
Every effort has been made by the Publishers to ensure that the websites in this book are suitable for children, that they are of the highest educational value, and that they contain no inappropriate or offensive material. However, because of the nature of the Internet, it is impossible to guarantee that the contents of these sites will not be altered. We strongly advise that Internet access is supervised by a responsible adult.

TIMELINE

632 The Holy Prophet Muhammad (pbuh) dies in Madinah, a desert city in Saudi Arabia. The first wars are waged by his father-in-law, Caliph Abu-Bakr.

711 Muslim soldiers conquer the Iberian peninsula – that's Portugal and Spain. They oust the ruling Visigoths from Cordoba.

752 Abbasid caliphs take over the Umayyads from their rule over Middle Eastern Islamic lands. Caliph al-Mansur makes Baghdad the region's capital.

756 Umayyad ruler, Abdul Rahman, creates an Umayyad Islamic state in Spain to rival the Abbasids in the Middle East.

762 Caliph al-Mansur begins to build the Abbasid capital in Baghdad.

767 An Islamic state is set up by Ibn Madrar at Sijilmasa in Africa.

786 Harun al-Rashid (reigned 786-809) becomes the Abbasid Caliph in Baghdad. He starts to build the House of Wisdom.

800 Algebra is invented by al-Khwarizmi, and science develops.

813 Al'Ma'mun (reigned 813-833), al-Rashid's son, finishes building the House of Wisdom. He gathers scientists and scholars, including Persians, Jews and Christians.

836 Abbasid caliphs move temporarily from Baghdad to a new capital, Samarra.

861 Turkish soldiers murder Caliph al-Mutawakkil, the ruler of Samarra, and disrupt the region until 945.

908 A weak Baghdadi ruler, al-Muqtadir, spends too much money and leads to the city's inevitable decline.

1258 Hulagu Khan and his Mongolian warriors sack Baghdad and destroy the House of Wisdom.

INDEX